dedication

For my Dad, who took my phone call and got me through the first hour.

For Claire, who sat with me and got me through the first night.

*For my Mum, my Aunty Christine, and my sister Emma, who got me through the funeral.
And who've held the line for me ever since.*

*For J.
The best person I ever met.*

A SMALL BOOK ABOUT SUICIDE. FOR THE MORNING AFTER
Copyright 2020 by **FIONA JEFFERIES**

All rights reserved. No part of this book may be used or reproduced in any manner whatsoever without written permission from **FIONA JEFFERIES**, except as provided by Australia copyright law or in the case of brief quotations embodied in articles and reviews.

This book addresses the delicate subject of suicide. If you are directly affected by the contents of this book we recommend you seek professional help.

The scanning, uploading and distribution of this book via the Internet or via any other means without the permission of the publisher is illegal and punishable by law.

Please purchase only authorised electronic editions and do not participate in or encourage electronic piracy of copyrighted materials. Your support of the author's rights is sincerely appreciated.

Printed in Australia
ISBN: 978-0-6485211-9-8 (sc)
ISBN: 978-0-6489733-0-0 (e)

First Printing: 2020

table of contents

	Introduction	04
CHAPTER ONE	Why Did They Suicide?	06
CHAPTER TWO	Getting Through the First 24 Hours	09
CHAPTER THREE	The Practical Part	16
CHAPTER FOUR	What You Might Be Feeling	19
CHAPTER FIVE	How You Can Handle the Confused, Angry and Absent	22
CHAPTER SIX	How to Take Care of Yourself After the Initial Body Shock	25
CHAPTER SEVEN	You Can Honour Them	29
CHAPTER EIGHT	How You Rejoin Life	31
CHAPTER NINE	The Gift of Suicide (Say What?)	34
CHAPTER TEN	So, You're Here Because You're Thinking of Killing Yourself	37
CHAPTER ELEVEN	The Story of J and I	39
CHAPTER TWELVE	Words From My Mum	41
CHAPTER THIRTEEN	Aunty Christine's Story	44
CHAPTER FOURTEEN	Emma's Story	47
CHAPTER FIFTEEN	Anon's Story	49
CHAPTER SIXTEEN	The "Suicide Slipstream" Checklist	52
	Acknowledgements: THANK YOUS AND LOVE LETTERS	57

introduction

I really wish you did not have to read this book. I'm thinking that you've not mistakenly picked this up over a Helen Garner tome and that you're here because you've lost a loved one through suicide.

I'm sorry.

I'm so sorry that you're going through this.

I want you to know that as devastated and untethered as you might be feeling right now, it won't be like this forever. You still have the white-hot anger, the despair, the heavy sadness and so many other feelings to move through.

As you move through all the feelings, I also know this to be true: you will get through it. You will find reasons to smile, laugh and wonder again. You'll find reasons to be delighted, to venture out in the world again, and to remember the person who took their own life with love.

But that's not now.

Right now, you're in the waiting room between what was and what now is —and that's a pretty fucked up space to be.

I'm hoping that this small, short book about suicide will be your companion through the vastness of the suicide slipstream and give you some comfort during this most wretched time.

I don't come to the topic of suicide through academia, scientific research or longitudinal studies of why people choose to take their own life. I got my invite to this very shitty party through a very dear and special person, who I loved deeply, taking his own life. In the aftermath of that incident when picking through the debris of my life, I went looking for other people's accounts of suicide and how they endured the unendurable. J's suicide took place in the years before peak internet, so personal stories of suicide were pretty light on. The internet has given rise to people sharing their stories of how they survived the suicide of a loved one and now I'm adding my voice to theirs. So, shout out to the age of the Interwebs! We not only get to watch adorable videos of dachshunds doing batshit crazy things and to read Henry Rollins blogs, we get to read or hear first person accounts of suicide survival.

As bleak as things are going to get through the suicide slipstream, where you will be pulled along by an event so awful you can barely conceive of it, I want you to hold the line.

And your line is this:

I will make meaning of this event.

And, I will grab onto every stick of hope and resilience I can like a motherfucker.

I will endure.

Please note: This is a personal account of suicide and not to be taken as professional advice. Some of this content may be triggering. If you are feeling anxious or depressed, please speak with your GP who can refer you to a professional to assist you further.

Chapter 1

why did they suicide?

It could be because they were tired of feeling like shit all the time and wanted it to end.

It could be that they thought they were a burden to others.

It could because of a catastrophic event in their life like the breakdown of a significant relationship, loss of a job or financial stress.

It could be that all hope for a better life was lost.

It could be they no longer wanted to live with the raw shame of sexual, emotional or physical abuse.
It could be because they were no longer able to withstand the online trolls and vicious criticism.
It could be because the meds no longer worked, and the emotional and physical pain is excruciating.
It could be because their support network of people has died or slipped from contact and they feel completely alone.

> THE HONEST AND HEARTBREAKING ANSWER IS THAT YOU'LL NEVER REALLY KNOW. EVEN IF YOUR LOVED ONE HAS LEFT A LETTER OR CALLED YOU BEFORE THEY ENDED THEIR LIFE, THE EXPLANATION THEY GIVE IS SO INCONSEQUENTIAL WHEN COMPARED AGAINST THE FINALITY OF SUICIDE.

J called me before he died.

And, he mailed a letter to his sister before he took his life. In the letter he very rationally stated his reasons for ending his life, much like you would set out an argument about why design is a triumph of form over function in an essay format, giving facts and supported reasoning. It was all so fucking benign if it was not for the end result of J extinguishing his own life. The thing that really stung was that J had struggled with crafting a structured essay at university, so I traded lessons in essay writing for lessons in using wood lathes and learning to weld. He then used those lessons I gave him to construct a well-reasoned argument for taking his own life, one that even I had to admire for its structure and adherence to tone.

> I ONLY READ THAT LETTER ONCE, AND I WANTED NO MORE OF IT.

Because how could the absolute finality of death be summed up in two and a half pages of cursive writing? For the first few weeks after I read the letter I had furious arguments with J in my head, rebutting each of his reasons to suicide. I even started writing my own essay back to him about the reasons to stay here, with me. But I was too raw in the slipstream of suicide and my writing was consumed with viciousness and vitriol as I tried to process so many emotions.

> SUICIDE AS DEATH IS UNIQUE.

Other deaths are explainable.

They died because of cancer.

They died because of old age.

They died because of blunt force trauma.

By being explainable, you have a focus and a place for your grief, anger and sadness. Suicide offers no such shelter. You can be angry, sad and grieving, but in the absence of having a villain to pin it on — cancer, a perpetrator, a speeding vehicle, something explainable — the one who suicided becomes the sole focus of your emotions. And when all your feelings are directed at the one who suicided, there are so many layers to the trauma of experiencing death.

I will try to save you from some emotional pain here and lovingly caution you against trying to have a perfectly understood and clear reason for why someone took their life. Even if there were letters sent, calls made, previous attempts to suicide … for you, there will be no reason sufficient or broad enough to explain the vast pit of pain experienced after losing someone to suicide.

Over time, you will become a detective as people offer stories about your loved one, some changes in behaviour they might have noticed, some things they did that were out of character. To that soupy emotional mix you will add your own observations that were off base about them, or perhaps that you were even blindsided by this act and saw no change or warning sign. From all this, you will fashion a partly completed sketch of their reasons, but to save yourself from going into the ever descending spiral of trying to figure out the reasons for them suiciding...there is no reason big enough to explain suicide.

You have to become a black belt ninja in being okay with uncertainty. You will never have the answers you so desperately desire. No news, explanation or item of discovery will fully colour in the sketch of why people take their own life. Get comfortable with the uncertainty and release yourself from fully understanding both the act and lead up. I found the less I focussed on the why and how, the more able I was to participate in my own grief rather than avoiding it by being a first-class detective. It's natural as humans to want to understand the inconceivable, but nothing in the realm of suicide makes logical sense. Take yourself out of the detective role and feel what you feel instead. By staying in the detective role, you're jammed up in your own head, replaying the lead-up loop of what they said, what they did, searching for any clues that you should have picked up that suicide was on the cards.

> TO ACCEPT UNCERTAINTY RELIEVES YOU OF THE ROLE AS DETECTIVE,
> AND BRINGS YOU
> FACE-TO-FACE WITH YOUR FEELINGS.

Chapter 2

getting through the first 24 hours

J had been missing for four days, his family thought there was a chance he might be on his way to visit me. I sat up, curtailed my time away from home and switched the outside light on when it got dark, only to turn it off again as morning rolled around and he had not shown.

> ON A FRIGID SUNDAY EVENING,
> HIS SISTER CALLED TO LET ME KNOW, HE'D BEEN
> FOUND IN HIS CAR,
> IN AN ISOLATED PART OF RURAL NEW SOUTH
> WALES,
> DEAD,
> PERHAPS FOR A NUMBER OF DAYS.

I asked the required questions of how she was (fucking terrible), how the rest of the family were (fucking shocked and unbelieving), and then thanked her for the call and hung up.

My first thought was *I'm not going to feel anywhere close to normal for fuck knows how long*, so I continued to work on a design project for another thirty minutes and refused the reality that J had taken his own life. Anytime my brain tried to process the news, I could see myself standing above a gaping pit of despair and then walking away from it saying, 'I can't. Not yet'.

After I hit save on the design, I powered down my computer, walked to the lounge and called my parents. Dad took the call. I'd hoped Mum might be the last person that I spoke to before normal evaporated as I was not sure Dad was up for the emotional task of bearing what I was about to dump onto his shoulders. But no, my Dad got the call where he heard his daughter totally break apart, howl like an animal and manage to choke out, 'The bastard's gone and done it … he's killed himself'.

And then I threw myself into that gaping pit of despair and stayed there for what seemed lifetimes.

> YOU WILL BE SO, SO RAW DURING THE FIRST TWENTY-FOUR HOURS.
>
> YOU'LL DRIFT BETWEEN THE WORLD OF WHAT WAS AND WHAT IS.

You'll be churning through emotions and thoughts:

I need to call my sister.

I think I need a sandwich.

Where's my car keys,
I'm going for a drive.

Oh, fuck no.

No.

No. No. NO. NO. NO.

If you're reading this and it's just twenty-four hours after the event. I don't want to add to the chaos that's already your reality, so let's keep this punchy.

It's okay to feel happy, sad, raging, hopeless all at the same time.
This is your new normal.

It's okay to feel nothing.
This is your new normal.

It's okay to vomit or want to eat.
This is your new normal.

It's okay to sleep or want to stare blankly at walls.
This is your new normal.

It's okay to want to talk about this or become mute with sadness.
This is your new normal.

> IN ESSENCE, WHATEVER YOU'RE FEELING WITHIN THE FIRST TWENTY-FOUR HOURS IS OKAY.

HERE'S SOME PRACTICAL HELP I'M OFFERING YOU FOR THE FIRST:

24 HOURS

Call a loved one who you know will be okay and not freaked out by a crisis and tell them about what happened and what you're feeling. I'd also suggest you preface the conversation with saying, 'This terrible thing has happened, and I just want to spill it all out, I'm not looking for solutions, I just want someone to witness this.'

And, then let it rip …

Say everything you're feeling, especially the stuff you do want to give words to like, 'I had a feeling she was going to do this.' Talk for as long or as short a time as necessary for you. Ask them to check up on you tomorrow.

Move your body. The soul quake that is suicide, will be an out of body experience, so spend just a little time either going for a short walk, doing some yoga or using a fitness app for cardio.

Eat a little something. Your internal nervous system has just been zapped, give it some sustenance to help you process what you're going through.

Call a trusted loved one or friend to come and be with you. I called my friend Claire after I had spoken to my parents and she dropped everything to sit with me, hold my hand and bear witness to my pain.

72 HOURS

For the initial few days after J died, I moved through life like a sleepwalker. Going to the newsagency to pick up art material for a design project I was working on, all I was focused on was getting through the next ten minutes. My parents had straightaway offered on the night of J's death to come and be with me and I had flatly refused, telling them I needed to prove to myself I could get through this.
Alone.

At night, I lay with the electric blanket on the highest setting, unable to warm myself. I was in shock. The following day, after deciding not to cancel a work meeting, I found myself driving en route to the meeting, and then suddenly shrieking as the knowledge set in that the steering wheel was one of the last things J saw before ending his life. Pulling over to the side of the road, panting, I called my Mum to talk me off the emotional cliff I was carefully clinging to.

> THESE EARLY DAYS POST SUICIDE ARE WHAT I TERM THE SUICIDE SLIPSTREAM.
> YOU DID NOT CREATE THE SUICIDE, BUT YOU GET CAUGHT UP IN ITS ALL-CONSUMING WAKE.

TO SURVIVE THE SLIPSTREAM, HELPFUL OFFERINGS

- Don't do as I did, and refuse offers of love and support. Say, yes!
- I hold few regrets, but if I had my time over I would have said a grateful 'yes, please' to my parents coming to stay with me, rather than toughing it out alone under the batshit crazy idea that I needed to prove I could get through it.
- Ask for help in telling others.
- The experience of telling others who need to know about the suicide is draining, get a phone tree happening so you don't relive the experience repeatedly and have to manage other people's reactions.
- Move, eat nutritious food, like you did in the first 24-hour period to sustain yourself.
- If you're able, write some thoughts and feelings down. Even if it sounds demented, angry or confused, it will help you process what you're going through

7 DAYS

J's funeral was held seven days after he died.

I drove to his rural home town.

Mum, my sister and aunty formed a support posse and met me at the highway motel where we were staying the night before the funeral. It was the first time I really let go and I was scooped up in their love. During the night, hearing me cry, my sister crawled out of her own bed and into mine to rub my back. My aunty, who had loved J and adored his spirit just hugged me, both of us in tears saying, 'There are no words… no words for this.'

At the funeral, with the priest talking of yokes and finally J finding the yoke of God's making, which was totally off base from J's own rejection of traditional Catholicism, Mum wrapped her arm firmly around my waist as I near wilted during the standing hymns.

'I can't do this …,' I whispered to her and she gripped me even tighter as if to slow my decent into the pit of despair.

The funeral is an obvious, outward marker that things have moved on.

People came together to grieve, share stories and offer support. After the funeral, everything recedes, and the expectation is that life will resume and return to its previous rhythm.

This is an outright falsehood and if anyone dares tell you, 'Well, you can get on with your life now', you're allowed to dick punch them. There's no normal for you.

Your life and soul have a hole punched through them and nothing can make that right. So many people around you will want you to resume life as before, but how can you when your heart has stopped beating?

> THE FUNERAL IS THE START,
>
> NOT THE END OF SURVIVING THE SLIPSTREAM,
>
> PREPARE YOURSELF FOR MAKING IT ACROSS THE
>
> BADLANDS.

People are naturally going to move on with their lives and resume normal transmission, so it's unfortunately on you to make sure you're getting the help you need. Ask those that you trust and who can support you in the way you need, to check in with you regularly and be okay with you not wanting to talk sometimes. Ask them to keep showing up for you and in return, please talk to them and share how you feel.

If you can, take some time out from school or work to take care of yourself.

Keep moving your body, eating well and writing out how you're feeling.

Gather together momentos, letters, voice recordings, keepsakes and other items to honour your loved-one's memory. This is not necessarily for now but for later when you have trouble remembering the exact sound of their voice, the smell of the inside of their leather jacket, or a shared selfie. A friend I went to university with who had endured the loss of so many loved ones passed on this hard truth, said as he lit the fourth cone of the day,

'Fiona, the worst part about death is not the loss of the person, it's the loss of memories.'

Think about it. How often do you sit with your mates or family and reminisce and laugh over old times, with each of you filling in for the other and building out the story? When someone dies, there is only you to act as keeper of the stories and memory is not a reliable device (this, from a fella who smoked four cones each day before he emerged from bed …), that's what you lose … the person and the memories.

Seek help from trusted friends if you need to close bank accounts, wrap up memberships, cancel drivers licences, and all the practical stuff that has to be taken care of when someone dies. Consider appointing a couple of personal powers of attorney (POAs) who will accompany you to meetings, or appointments, or sit with you as you navigate this as sometimes you'll be weeping on the phone to an overseas call centre operator who is flummoxed at your muffled words. Time to hand the receiver over to the POA who will take over the enquiry while you retreat to the lounge.

What I found helpful, no matter what stage of grief I was working through, was to concentrate on getting through the next ten minutes, or the next hour, or the next day. When you're grieving and managing waves of emotions, if you can just focus on getting through the next chunk of time, it becomes much more manageable than wondering hopelessly how you're going to get through the next year feeling so devastated.

No matter what stage of the grieving process you're going through, please reach out for support, love and care. People aren't always intuitive and might be thinking (and hoping) you're doing better than you are.

Use your words, hold that line.

Chapter 3

the practical part

When my grandad, was in hospital with his organs slowly shutting down, he told Mum 'There's nothing easy about dying.' Grandad could also have been referring to the aftermath of death, too.

Depending on where you live and your relationship to the person who suicided, the following list might be relevant to you. Regardless, it's a checklist of sorts to guide you in the fog of grief.

Most likely, the police will be involved if there's suicide involved.

It's tough for them and you. Treat them with care and answer any questions they have with as much information as possible. Don't be fussed if you're a hot mess of tears and tissues, they are used to this. Have a support person with you and keep yourself as calm as possible.

There'll probably be a coroner involved, as well, when the cause of death is a suspected suicide. Don't freak out at this. It is a totally normal part of determining official cause of death—the coroner's office is used to dealing with the loved ones of someone who's taken their own life—you're in a safe space and the coroner will often have support services for the bereaved. Always grab that offer of help and assistance to help you navigate the aftermath of suicide.

There may be a Will or maybe there won't. Check with the lawyer, solicitor, attorney of the loved one to establish what might be in place. If you're not the next of kin tasked with sorting this, it's a generous act of love to contact the person who is and offer help with enacting of the Will. The very last thing anyone needs when in the throes of grief is a stack of paperwork and legal documents to wrap their head around. Be of help if you can.

Sometimes there is a funeral plan in place and other times, you've got to organize this on the run. Some life advice for anyone reading this, get your Will and funeral plan wish-list in order—no matter what age you are, especially—if you're fitter than a Mallee bull. Don't put your loved ones through the task of selecting caskets from a catalogue in a room with far too many velvet curtains and a sweaty funeral director, trying to weigh up if your life's value is best represented by the $6,000 timber polished casket or if you really need to go out in style in the $10K white glossy casket with more bling than Liberace. If there is no funeral plan in place or no wishes left behind, just do your best. Really, it doesn't matter if you mistakenly picked "Bridge Over Troubled Water" for the funeral procession and you realize six weeks later your loved one hated Simon and Garfunkel. In a lot of ways, the funeral is not for the person departed but for those left behind.

There is a laundry list of things that need to be wrapped up like bank accounts, gym memberships, licences, work swipe cards, digital subscriptions, utilities billing, home ownership, rental premises, owned businesses, superannuation, death benefits, credit cards, insurances … so many. If you're the next of kin, for the love of all things holy, divvy the list up between trusted supporters so you don't bear the responsibility of having to repeat the story of why you're wanting to close this account, that subscription, the email service. In some ways the move to an automated system is a good thing in this instance. In many cases you can simply do a copy and paste message to the provider and then let them sort it out from there with the follow up delegated to a trusted supporter. If you aren't the next of kin or POA, please offer assistance to those that are. This is a deeply overwhelming time and to manage grief along with the sheer mind-bending frustration of a call centre is often a bridge too far. Please be a good person and offer any assistance you feel comfortable in providing.

Gather keepsakes and mementos. Your first instinct might be to burn the whole thing to the fucking ground to thank them for the turmoil you're now in, but this is for your future self and those who loved the departed.

Write your feelings out. If only so they're not swimming about your head. You can also revisit your notes in the weeks and months to come to show you how far you've come since the days of continual weeping, and that yes, you are making a life from the new normal.

For me, I found it really helpful to have something practical to focus on that could distract me from the churn of emotions. You might be the type of person to really get a sense of achievement ticking things off lists and if so, embrace this way of working through grief. If you're overwhelmed by the tasks that need to be handled or want to avoid the finality of closing bank accounts at this tender time, then that's okay too. Do what you feel you can, seek assistance from friends and family and address what you need to later when you feel able.

Chapter 4

what you might be feeling

THE CALL I RECEIVED FROM J WAS NOTHING AND EVERYTHING.

'Hi Fiona, it's J.
Pause.
Pause.
Pause.
Just calling…, *(pause)* to see how you are?
Pause.
Pause.
Pause.
Anyway, catch up soon.'

I was out at the time rowing and his missed call recorded on my answering machine. He left no number and did not call back. In the days afterwards, assembling the pieces of the jigsaw that were J's last hours, we feel that J wrote a final letter to his sister, posted it and called me en route to the cold, dark hill where he took his life.
I have to say the unsayable here and admit that J's suicide was not a total surprise. I knew that this was one of many paths his life could take. But in knowing that suicide could be an option for him, I also carried the guilt of not doing more to avoid the outcome of suicide for J.

Perhaps you're feeling the same, guilty that you were not able to do more to help your loved one choose a different path from suicide. Maybe through conversations and the way the person behaved over the years, you knew they had been considering suicide. Or, it could be that there were a number of suicide attempts—now, this last attempt was successful—in the worst possible way. Maybe you are exhausted from previous attempts and although this was another cry for help, you didn't respond quickly or firmly enough and they're … dead. Gone for good.

Suicide brings up so many feelings and a lot of them are difficult to navigate and bear. I have heard (quietly) from other people who've lost someone through suicide that there's sometimes even relief when an attempt on life is successful, that they can finally stop living on the edge, their life having previously been eclipsed by the person repeatedly attempting to take their life and all the drama that swirls around that.

Guilt.

Relief.

Sadness.

Anger.

Despair.

Hopelessness.

Fear.

All these feelings, are completely valid in the suicide slipstream.

Don't dampen them down.

Or attempt to talk yourself out of *feeling* what you're *feeling*.

I found it helpful to think of emotions like a (very fucking heavy) bag. Each day, I reached for a different bag and then put it down for a break. I could determine how long the break was, and then I could choose to pick it up again or pick another emotion, even the forgiveness bag, for the smallest amount of time. I'd drop that bag of forgiveness like it was hot—as I wasn't able to be all forgiving and loving in the early stages post J's death—then I'd pick up the anger bag and haul that about. I found visualization really helpful as it gave me a chance to separate myself (Fiona) from the emotion (hopelessness) and be able to function for periods of time on daily tasks like run my business and see clients before I loaded up that bag and dragged it around again.

One night a week after J died, I was raging around the house, talking to him furiously. At one point through tears and hurt, I said to him, 'Why didn't you tell me about how you were feeling? Why couldn't you do that? Even if it was not me, it could have been your sister, or even … Lifeline.' I stormed towards the phone, dramatically dialled the number for Lifeline (a 24-hour fully-staffed call line for people either thinking of taking their life, or going through a traumatic time and not sure where to seek help, or for those bereaved and having trouble coping) and then heard … the engaged signal. I bust out laughing, seeing the black humour, telling J he could call a suicide prevention hotline and for it to be engaged. So humour—even coloured black—can be something that you feel, and it doesn't indicate that you don't love them or respect the gravity of the situation but that you're instead a human who is able to express any and all emotions.

> PLEASE DON'T CENSOR YOURSELF AS YOU GRIEVE, TELLING YOURSELF YOU SHOULDN'T FEEL SOME HEAVY EMOTIONS.
> BE KIND TO YOURSELF, FEEL WHAT YOU FEEL, THERE WILL BE A TIME WHERE YOU FEEL ON STEADIER EMOTIONAL GROUND.
> BUT NOT YET, SO TREAD WITH CARE.

CHAPTER 5

the confused, angry & absent

I had a tarot reading from a woman in a suburban shopping centre about six months after J's death as I was so desperate for answers and resolution. Fanning the cards out on a rickety wooden table, our space barely cloaked from the rest of the new age shop with a dolphin patterned curtain, she consulted the cards while my shaking voice told her I was there for some answers about J's death. Nodding, looking at the cards she told me offhand, 'You know, if he really loved you, he would have never killed himself.'

When I saw Dad two weeks after J's death, he hugged me and as I slumped against him, barely able to carry my own weight, he said, 'At least now you can get on with your life.'

Then, a few months after J's death, I met for lunch with a dear friend and as tears sprang up for no reason, she said, 'Oh … I thought you'd be over this by now.'

Yes.
You're going to hear a lot of fucked up shit when you're in the suicide slipstream.
My friend and my dad had the very best of intentions. The tarot reader, well, the jury is out on anyone plying their trade behind a dolphin printed curtain in a suburban shopping centre.

Everyone that comes into contact with you will be scratching about, trying to find words to express their sympathy, sorrow and disbelief. Because they're scratching about they sometimes collect the wrong words and often say unthoughtful things that add exponentially to your pain.

People might speak with anger about your loved one, express confusion and even be MIA during your suicide slipstream. They will say all things to you with your broken heart and shattered spirit and will look for answers from you, as perhaps you were closer to the departed loved-one or witnessed their final hours or took delivery of their final words. It can be particularly hurtful when friends who were previously staunch supporters and visibly present in your life, drift from sight and aren't available to you for support.

Finding meaningful things to say and being comforting is tricky enough when a death has occurred. Overlay the complexity of feelings following a suicide on an already troubled time, and no ideal outcome is possible.

When I heard people say things that stabbed at my wounded heart, or I looked again at my answering machine longing for a call back from a friend who didn't know what to say, I tried to remember that they were doing their best in challenging times. My friend had not known J but she could see the pain I was in and not having lost someone to suicide at that point in her life, she wasn't to know there was no divine timeline to resuming life. My dad had known and loved J as first my friend, and then partner, so while he was telling me I could now get on with my life free from the question of J being in it, I had to pause and remember he was going through a shitty time himself.

We've all been stuck for the right words to say when we meet someone grieving and, in the rush, to say something … anything …. the intent is compassion, but the execution can be painful. I think the most honest thing I've ever said about death was to my friend Shirley who lost her mum suddenly and without warning. At the funeral, I gripped Shirley and said through streams of tears, 'I'm so, so sorry, this is totally fucked what you and your family are going through.'

Feel free to steal this and omit/insert swear words as the situation demands. On the night when J died, Claire came over to be with me through those first awful, terrible hours, the gift she gave me was presence.

Perhaps it was because Claire had lost her dad only a few years before and the things that helped her during the grieving process were still fresh. Claire sat next to me on the lounge as I reached for tissue after tissue soaking them with tears and snot, saying nothing, just holding my hand with tears in her eyes. It's not easy to sit with someone in their grief and if you can manage it, I would encourage you to do so.

> NO WORDS ARE NEEDED,
> NOT PLATITUDES LIKE THINGS WILL GET BETTER,
> OR THERE'S A REASON FOR THIS.
> JUST PRESENCE,
> COMPASSION,
> PERHAPS, SOME HOT TEA
> AND SOME DARK CHOCOLATE.

People aren't going to say the things you desperately want to hear; that it has all been a badly thought out joke and your loved one is not really dead ... in fact, surprise! Here they are now! So, with that, anything said by anyone will never measure up. Try to remember that most people are trying to offer comfort and it can come out poorly, so soak up the intent and not necessarily the actual words.

There will be some people close to you who will exit your life either temporarily or permanently—the rawness and realness of your pain is too much for them to bear witness to—they don't feel they can offer anything of comfort.

I know you're already going through so much but have a generous spirit to those fumbling with words, offers of help and hope during this sensitive time. There's no cheat sheet or on-line manual, for this everyone is doing their best to support and love you even though it may not be in the way you want or need.

Chapter 6
how to take care of yourself after the initial body shock

As minutes become hours, hours become days, days become weeks and the months pass, time post-suicide can become reimagined. Time slows down so much, it feels like you could count each individual breath, especially during the slow drag of the night. You notice time by the moving forward and back through the stages of grief: disbelief, anger, bargaining, depression and then acceptance. It's a mistake to think the progression through these stages is linear. It more resembles spaghetti thrown at the wall where it's a tangled mess, stages overlapping and surging ahead and then regressing backward.

I would love to give you a perfectly coloured GANT chart for the period you'll be grieving with tabs showing the stages and expected duration, but the truth is, the experience of losing someone is deeply personal and everyone navigates it uniquely.

I will tell you that you'll feel like you're in shock for a long time.
You may feel cold or hot intensely,
you may involuntary shake no matter what the climate.
You'll find it difficult to focus on mundane tasks,

SMALL TALK WILL MAKE YOU WANT TO PEEL YOUR SKIN OFF.
YOU MAY CRY FOR NO REASON, OR FEEL SO NUMB, YOU WON'T BE ABLE TO SUMMON ANY EMOTION.
YOU MAY SLEEP FOR LONG PERIODS TO ESCAPE THE MAELSTROM,
OR YOU MIGHT TREAD THE FLOOR HOUR AFTER HOUR SEEKING SLEEP.

ALL THESE BEHAVIOURS ARE VALID AND WITHIN THE REALM OF EXPECTATIONS,
PLEASE DON'T BE PANICKED,
YOU MAY EXPERIENCE THEM MONTHS OR YEARS AFTER YOUR LOVED ONE HAS DIED.

The only time I felt relief from the slipstream of suicide was immediately upon waking—those small moments leaving sleep when my consciousness fired up—I forgot for the briefest time, J had died.

As my senses came too, reality poured in.
He was forever dead.
And, I eased myself back into the slipstream.

I've advocated previously about writing about how you're feeling and what you're experiencing as a way of processing the grief. I also strongly suggest you talk to friends and family as well. In most cases, your friends and family will have known the loved one and will be grieving alongside you, perhaps not with the same intensity, or even at the same stage. I have to acknowledge here that there are limits to the support your loved ones can provide. If exchanges are leaving you calmer, more supported or even have a neutral effect, these are fine to seek out again in the future. If you're feeling more turbulent or upset from the conversation, it's time to look for someone else to talk with, perhaps a professional counsellor or psychologist who has training in supporting the bereaved.

Everyone comes to suicide from their own angle. I had to recognize that having regular conversations with a family member of J's was not helping me move forward. Despite our intense love of J, we were at different stages of grief and working through tough memories. I was feeling intensely guilty that I had come to think in the past few years that suicide could have been an option for J and that I did not do more. The family member had never dreamed that J could do this, so our memories and experience of J were opposed and neither of us could get the support from the other that we needed.

It's okay to step back from conversations that are increasing your pain rather than offering some relief. I found it helpful to seek assistance from a counsellor specializing in grief at the first-year anniversary of J's death and then some sixteen years later, I've now found a psychologist who can help me unpack the residual grief and the patterns I developed in the time since the suicide. There's no standard here, you can only be honest about how you feel and what you need. Try to avoid anything that numbs you out like drugs, alcohol, dangerous behaviours and reach instead for support and understanding to move you out of the slipstream and to safer shores. Don't be afraid to try a few different professionals until you find someone you feel comfortable talking to and who will offer you a plan to feel more in control of your life. It can take a number of goes until you land the professional that is right for you. I can't oversell the benefit of using a professional skilled in suicide bereavement. Family and friends aren't to be discounted but they have a vested interest in you. To have someone to speak with who is separate to the event and can offer impartial advice and observations is so helpful in your making sense of the trauma.

No suggestion about this at all, I'm telling you straight out—you need to tell people what you need both in the initial and latter stages of grief. It's going to be confronting telling people outright how they can best support you, but it's about love—both for yourself, and those who want to help. Rather than people gathering around you and making you feel so fragile that you'll shatter—tell them you'd love space and it's best to contact you on the phone. If you want around the clock support, ask a trusted loved one to move in. If you want to gather those who're also grieving to share memories and stories, send the invitations and buy snacks. People around you want to help and can sometimes be stuck for the best way to do that, without adding to your grief, so help them and yourself.

USE YOUR WORDS.
ASK FOR WHAT YOU NEED.

Don't worry if you need to change your mode of support mid-grief. What might have worked in the early stages of the shock, say a bunch of support on speed dial, might now irritate you in the slipstream of suicide and now you really want less talk and have more personal reflection. It's cool.

> WHATEVER YOUR WOUNDED HEART
> AND SPIRIT CALLS FOR, ASK FOR THAT.

Please don't get stuck in the slipstream or think you can manage these complex emotions by yourself. Emotional isolation is sometimes what got your loved one to take their own life.

You are precious.

You matter.

Please, don't go that same way.

Reach out.

Seek professional help.

Be kind to yourself.

Isolation has no place here, soften and begin to heal.

CHAPTER 7

you can honour them

Remember the part in an earlier chapter when I told you not to set fire to all the photos, keepsakes and mementos you have of the person who took their life? Yeah, this is why. Because, at some point, you will find a new normal where you can think of them and smile or laugh and not want to murder them for killing themselves (only people losing a loved one to suicide will get the ridiculousness of that statement).

Once you've concluded the funeral and you've drifted in the suicide slipstream you might want to think of ways you can keep their memory alive. There will be a time in the future where you're less tender than you are now. Memories can be unreliable and fleeting so gather what you feel comfortable retaining and find a place for it. It also helps if you can draw meaning from the finality of suicide. By creating meaning, you're giving your rational mind something to land on, so it doesn't go skipping about for yonks replaying the worst memories.

SOME IDEAS ON CREATING MEANING FOR THIS CATASTROPHIC EVENT

- Make a donation or start a charitable foundation in their name that would support the values they held dear.
- Award a scholarship in a subject area they excelled in.
- Set up a shrine with images, words and special keepsakes to reflect on.
- Write the story of you and them.
- Plant a tree or donate a park bench in their honour.
- Write a song, poem, paint a picture, that invokes their memory.
- Live your best life and be grateful you have a chance to do things they didn't.

- Volunteer for a cause that was close to their heart.
- Do some activities you know they had planned in the future.
- Complete some of their unfinished projects.

Please don't launch into this list as a means for avoiding your pain or even while you're feeling particularly vulnerable. The function of honour is best done when you're feeling emotionally stable as the process will dredge up many feelings, and you don't want to set yourself back in the suicide slipstream.

Check in with yourself, do as much or as little as you feel able and don't feel obligated to do all or anything on this list, it's a suggestion sheet only. Pick something that has resonance for you. Ultimately, the practice of honour is for you, just as much as it is for your loved one, so make it as enjoyable as possible under the circumstances—not a form of punishment.

I honour J in the way I altered my life approach.
J had such an adventurous spirit.

He loved getting under the hood of things and tinkering about. One time, he designed and built his own on-land windsurfer and careered all over his family farm. I don't have this same fearlessness. I'm cautious and my mind goes to the worst-case scenario. Since J died, I've tried to develop a more fearless spirit and said yes to rowing 46 kilometres when the most I'd rowed continuously was 17 kilometres. I've said yes to growing my business and employing staff. I've said yes to opening my heart and risking hurt by dating again. I've said yes to travelling to places by myself and sparking conversations with strangers.

However, you choose to mark the life of your loved one, make it something meaningful to you. Something that will bring comfort when the pain flares up years down the track. Something you can return to when memories get sketchy. Something that marks the life of that special someone and says that they mattered, and they were loved.

CHAPTER 8
how you rejoin life

The aim here is for you to move out of the flow of the suicide slipstream and find your way to solid shores. When I think back to the immediate aftermath, and the months after J took his life, I can only describe it as being in the slipstream of the event. I felt I was trapped in the undertow and I was pulled along by an event totally outside my control and reasoning. Being tugged along in its wake, there were times when I felt I was going under, desperately reaching out to grab onto something tangible to stop myself from drifting further.

> THE SUICIDE SLIPSTREAM IS FUCKED.
> YOU PASS BY PEOPLE ON THE SHORELINE GOING
> ABOUT THEIR NORMAL LIVES,
> AND ALL YOU CAN DO IS WATCH
> AS YOU TUMBLE, RICOCHETING ABOUT
> IN THE SLIPSTREAM.

There'll be a time where the pull of the slipstream is lessened, where its grip relaxes and the strong currents ebb. This will be the sign for you to start creating a new life for yourself without the physical presence of your loved one in it.

Go slowly here.
Don't rush at it.
You've been through a life changing event.
I'd warn against making major life decisions like beginning or ending a

relationship, selling homes or possessions, moving, dumping a career or engaging in what might be viewed as risky activities. Grief can flatten your emotions, so you no longer experience the highs or lows and so to jolt your emotions back to registering, you might be considering doing big shit.

Please pause.
Think this out before diving headlong into big events.
Especially, if your motivator is to feel some emotion ... any emotion.

I reckon I took a good year of sliding along in the suicide slipstream before I waded to firmer ground. The catalyst was a letter from my Mum. Since I'd moved away from home after university, she'd write me letters, filling me in on home life and what the idiot neighbours were up to (Scandalous!). A letter arrived for me about a year after J died and it began: Fiona, you don't seem like yourself.
Fuck, no, I did not, I did not feel anything.
And, that realisation was what prompted me to seek counselling sessions for bereavement. I thought I'd been doing okay but when Mum had that "come to Jesus" moment, I saw myself through the eyes of another. And I was sinking in that slipstream.

Over time, I've also done other things to rejoin life. I joined a gym to move the energetic remains of the raw grief. I started saying yes to going out with friends rather than begging off. I dated again. I'd been lucky that I had kept my fledgling business ticking on, but I took the next step in ditching the side gig of Borders shop assistant to pursue my business dream full time.

And, in the years after that again,
I moved to Sydney to be closer to my family.
I started rowing again and found my lady posse on the Lane Cover River.
I had a long-term relationship.
I travelled widely.
I held my nieces for the first time and promised to be the best Aunty Panther, and that they could count on me for love, support and worship of rock and roll, always.
I bought my apartment in Sydney.
I grew my business so that it employs women in a traditional male field.
I've redesigned my life.

This list is not exhaustive, but the effect is to show you that life—even one that differs so greatly to the one you imagined with your loved one in it—goes on ... It's not worse or better, just different and it is up to you how you make it meaningful for yourself.

As you build your new life, there will be things lost to you: close friends or family members might have drifted from your life—hobbies that might have once sparked joy leave you bored. Places you loved to visit are tedious: even treasured possessions have lost their allure. Nothing to be alarmed about here. You've transformed through the experience of suicide and not everything is transferable into your new life. I'd been out rowing when J called me before he took his life so when I went back to rowing a month after his death, I was dry heaving in the car park before our night-time rowing session. I'd finally found my sport of choice—when I'd moved to Melbourne some eight years before—exercising while sitting down, HAZZAH! Which also bought a bunch of amazing friends into my life. Now, on a frigid night on the Albert Park Lake I was in the grip of a full-blown panic attack, furious with myself that while I was out rowing J was already driving towards that lonely hill in rural New South Wales to affix a hose to his exhaust pipe, climb into his station wagon and let fumes fill the car and poison him to death. I gave up rowing that night when I tried unsuccessfully to claim remnants of my life pre-suicide slipstream. It took a move to a different state and five years before I got back on the water and fell back in love with rowing.

I've warned above about making sudden, jolting life changes when you lose someone to suicide, but you can also use it as a catalyst to pursue interests or make positive life changes that you might not have done otherwise. Losing someone you love to suicide throws into sharp relief the fragility of life and how quickly it can be cut short. While I ditched rowing for a time, I joined a gym which did not involve exercising while sitting down and signed up for yoga classes which helped calm the swirling thoughts in my head. I had given up thinking that I'd travel one day; now I made definite plans to travel, first to Perth over Christmas and then New Zealand at Easter.

Your life does not stop when theirs does.

You owe it to yourself and your loved one to live a life that is the best you're able to make it. You will find yourself from time to time back in the suicide slipstream, but the periods will be shorter and less intense.

CHAPTER 9

the gift of suicide (say what?)

I promise you, I've not lost my mind in saying that there's a gift in suicide. The loss of a loved one to suicide is going to mean so many different things to each person touched by it and none is right or wrong. I know there were many of J's friends and family who believed there were diverse and numerous reasons for J taking his own life and who's to say who nailed the exact reason—we don't have J on this spiritual plane to grill him about his reasons.

I can only share what's true for me. After what seemed like several lifetimes of reflection and countless boxes of tissues and tubs of Sara Lea ice cream, what J's death meant for me was that he could no longer carry the weight of his emotional pain and chose to end his life. Hope had dissolved and all he could see ahead of him was more suffering and pain. I think he felt like he was a burden to his loved ones and that our lives would be markedly improved if he was not around for us to worry over, trying to find ways to best support him when we didn't know precisely what was causing him so much grief.

My Mum and I have had regular conversations (Hey! Come around for happy hour sometime!) over the years about euthanasia and Mum is crystal clear about when it comes to her time, she doesn't want to linger, she wants a say in her treatment and care. And she wants it all done with. Awesome. Her choice and I fully support it. So, if I'm all about Mum's right to determine how the end of her life is played out … I couldn't carry the anger and anguish I had for J's having the same determination of his end of life path.

To be clear …
I'm not saying that suicide and euthanasia are the same thing and if laws

get up in Australia to allow people a say on their right to die and how they are cared for, it shouldn't lead to acceptance of a tragically high suicide rate in Australia and most first world countries.

But.
But.
But.

If I support euthanasia and the right for people to choose when the quality of life has diminished to the extent that there's no reasonable chance of improvement or stabilisation … then I also accept J's choice in deciding that the burden of the emotional and mental pain was too great to continue on, no matter how much I vehemently disagree with that same conclusion.

For all the fuzzy logic that might be housed in my rationalisation of suicide alongside euthanasia, what is important is where that brought me. As I carved out a place of acceptance for J's decision, it also allowed me to forgive him for leaving me and forgive myself for not doing more to drag out of him what was causing him so much grief. Forgiveness is so important in reclaiming your life and moving out of the suicide slipstream. While despair, sadness and anger flare up, the intensity lessens and the gaps between being okay and not are widened with the overlay of forgiveness.

For me, the forgiveness of J happened in the first year. For my own forgiveness, it took ages. Initially, I was not even aware I held such intense anger at my inability to dig deeper into what was behind his unexplained absences in my life and then how to find solutions that did not include ending his life. I felt complicit, especially when one of my first thoughts when I heard he had suicided was, Yes, that was an outcome I had dreaded. If I knew that, why didn't I do more? A lot of time post J's death was spent forgiving myself for not having the information I had now.

I'd really encourage you to forgive yourself too, for your own perceived complicity, shortcomings, lack of action, absence and whatever myriad failings you are beating yourself up about. Forgiveness is essential for you to live a full life. It will also move you towards the real gift of suicide, which is unconditional love. Once the anger dissolved and I had forgiven J and made a fragile but holding peace with myself, all that remained and always will is the unconditional love I had and have for him. It's a revelation to have such strongly coloured emotions settle into the soft hue of unconditional love.

NO PAIN,
NO ANGER,
NO HOPELESSNESS,
JUST LOVE, PURE LOVE.

Now don't get crazy, it's not all sunshine and fluffy bunny rabbits each and every day ... but, there is a lasting peace and a sense of love you have for your loved one that sits above the flare ups of confusion and grief.

FOR ME, THAT'S THE REAL GIFT OF SUICIDE.
TO LOVE SOMEONE DEEPLY,
WITHOUT JUDGEMENT DESPITE THE GAPING HOLE THEY HAVE LEFT IN YOUR LIFE.
TO FORGIVE THEM, NO MATTER WHAT THE FINAL YEARS AND MOMENTS HELD.
TO FORGIVE YOURSELF FOR BEING IMPERFECT BUT TRYING YOUR BEST.
TO HOLD THEM IN YOUR HEART FOREVER.

CHAPTER 10

so, you're here because you're thinking of killing yourself

It was not lost on me that with a title like this, it might pique the curiosity of someone looking to take their own life.

So if this is you I hope you make a different, better choice than suicide.

I don't know what's brought you to this place where you feel suicide is the only or best option. I can't tell you in all honesty that it will get better because I don't know. It's pretty condescending for me to trot out bumper sticker affirmations like 'It will get better' and 'Ask for help!' to someone who has battled chronic pain, illness or wrestled with dark thoughts for years.

But, I can tell you this.
The lives of your loved ones will be forever diminished by your death.
We'll agonise that we were not able to help you and see how badly you were suffering.
We'll feel guilty that we failed to see the signs or torture ourselves wishing we could have done more or spoken to you outright about what you were enduring.

We'll wonder how you would have been years on, how you would have loved a movie, a song, a view of the sea.

There will be profound sadness around birthdays, celebrations and special days because you're not there.

You'll be thought of constantly and loved deeply but you will be so missed and the lives of the ones you leave behind will be altered in ways you can't predict.

We aren't freed from the burden of you when you take your life, the burden shifts over to us and we carry it along with our love for you.

Then there's the stories of those who have survived suicide and overwhelmingly their last thoughts before the expected death were not of relief but, oh crap…I can't undo this, or regret. There's a very sobering read titled "Jumpers" on the New York Times website that talks about people who've jumped off the Gold Gate Bridge in San Francisco attempting to take their life and the line burns hard when a survivor talks about how all their problems were fixable … that is, right until they jumped. Read that article. It's harrowing but so insightful. Of course, you can't know for sure that your last thoughts will be of the sinking realisation that you can't undo this and really, things could turn around. But you also can't know for sure that they won't be.

What if you gave it one more day?
One more try?
One more reach out for help that can make a difference?

If you're thinking of *suicide*.

Please, take another day to think about it.

You are loveable, and worthy, and valuable, and have so much to contribute to the world and people around you.

Please make another choice.

Please give us another chance, the people who love and care for you, to help and support you.

Please pause.
Think this out before diving headlong into big events that can't be undone.

CHAPTER II

the story of J & I

I've not used J's full name, as I've not been able to get his sign off on his agreement to participate in my story ... the hotline to his spiritual plane seems to be on the fritz right now. And, I also think the privacy of his family and friends needs to be respected.

We met at university and from the very first day, I was amused by this stocky country boy in shorts, work boots and bushie's hat, strolling confidently into class. The amusement lasted the entire time I knew J, he was just a delight to be around. Even my uncle who had only met J a few times at family celebrations was forced to lean his weight against the kitchen bench to stop himself from collapsing when he heard of J's suicide ... the thought of such a vibrant, confident, funny and endearing bloke taking his own life just wasn't right for my uncle. This type of reaction was typical when the news of J's death passed around. People who had met J only a few times were touched by his interest in them and his easy presence, and were floored by the manner of his death ... what was he battling with that claimed him?

We got to know each other slowly through an exchange of skills. I knew how to write essays, crafting balanced arguments with the proper annotations and he knew how to weld, turn wood, fibreglass, fold metal, and do pretty much anything he put his mind to. He was a proper bastard like that ... so talented ... able to pull anything apart, understand how it works and then put it back together. He spent a lot of time at my place during the four years of university, welcomed by my family, fed by my mother, from the freezer and packet mixes but with so much love. He taught my sister how to dance, picked her up from her Thursday night late shift and talked to her as a person. He was respectful around my dad and talked to him about business and politics. He tolerated the borrowed cat from next door. He charmed us all and broke our hearts when he died.

We did not become partners until our final year of university—three years of friendship transformed into something even more amazing the night of my 21st birthday—from there, it was just a dream being his girlfriend.

We separated at the end of university but stayed together despite our different locations with me moving to the Gold Coast and J back to the farm. We stayed together until darkness and distance crept in. From there my 20s were marked by us being together and ridiculously happy, making plans for the future, and then the sense of unease and hopelessness J felt became overwhelming and he broke it off.

Together and then apart, together and then apart.
It was emotional hell for me, and then I decided to end it once and for all.

I was bereft and of course that became the perfect time to take up with someone else and become engaged because nothing says, 'no more' like an engagement ring. But soon enough that faltered as J had claimed my heart and there was nothing to share for another. We had established contact again and had one of the best conversations of our relationship, late one cold Autumn night, on the phone. We rambled over old and new ground for over five hours, both of us reluctant to hang up the phone.

This felt like a new start.
I remember thinking, He sounded so good. So good.

He was dead not five weeks later.
He was good because he'd made peace with his decision to end his life. He did not want to get off the phone as he knew this would be the last time he talked to me.

And, meanwhile I'd been planning how the next stage of our relationship would play out. J's death impacted my life in so many ways and changed it irrevocably, not always for the best. But, I would not have traded any of that pain and despair for the eleven beautiful, magical years, I had with J.
HE WAS BEAUTIFUL AND PERFECT AND MINE.

I'M SO GRATEFUL I HAD HIM FOR AS LONG AS I DID.

THE LOVE HE GAVE ME FOR THOSE ELEVEN YEARS WAS ENOUGH TO HELP ME RIDE OUT THE SUICIDE SLIPSTREAM AND ENDURES EVEN NOW.

I love you, J.

Chapter 12

words from my mum

On the advice of the lovely Alex who was the first person to read this book and say, 'Keep going, this could help someone,' I decided to include other people's experiences of suicide. But where to start? You just can't rock up to someone in the queue for cheesecake and say, 'Oh, looky at that Caramel swirl cheesecake … and hey, have you got a suicide story you could share?'

After twisting myself up, wondering how to approach this, the obvious solution to the problem made me smack my own forehead. I had suicide stories on tap. I had my family.

I spoke nervously to Mum first, telling her it was an offer only, totally cool if she wanted to take a pass but having her share something of her perspective would be gratefully received, not only by me, but perhaps someone else reading this, maybe they would see something in Mum's own words.

A week later, a series of pages pulled from an exercise book in Mum's beautiful cursive writing were shoved in my handbag during a visit to her and Dad. I pulled those notes from my bag later that night when I was back home and, well, what she wrote on those pages will be in my treasure box forever. Reading what she went through and what went on while I was deep in my own grief floored me. When you lose someone to suicide your life is fragmented and over time you claim bits of yourself back. But you're not the same as before, you're a new version assembled from those fragments. My Mum gave me back a big fragment when she wrote these words. Her experience also shows that the fallout from someone's suicide impacts so many, everyone shatters and tries to make sense of the finality of the act.

But also: there is love, so much love.

A phone call from Fiona changed our lives.
'Why?'
We were totally shocked, we were thinking,
'No, this has not happened.'
The immediate need for me to get to Melbourne to support Fiona.
(Fiona's Dad Graeme and I lived in Newcastle at the time.)
Graeme booked train travel for me, but Fiona said, 'don't come', she needed to figure out how to get through it by herself.
'Why,' we asked ourselves again and again.
It was a mistake.
Total confusion, there was no reasoning to this tragedy.
'Why,' repeated over and over again.
This wonderful young man had entered our lives and we all loved him.
It all felt like a horrible dream.
Phone calls were made back and forth to Fiona, her younger sister Emma, my parents, my sister Christine and my brother Geoffrey.
Everyone was deeply shocked and saddened.
J had been part of their lives as well.
He had become part of our family.
To our entire family he was a most special young man and the extended family as well.
My dad, 'Hugh Grandad', when told of J's suicide said,
'I can't believe it, not J … what about Fiona?'
My brother Geoffrey who's not an emotional person was totally floored,
'How's Fiona?'

Questions, questions. But no answers.
It could not happen to J.
He was a country boy at heart when he joined our family.
This affected many more people that J would have imagined.
The sadness was overwhelming for us.
We all muddled on until the funeral.
My sister Christine and I travelled to Orange to pick up Emma to then make the saddest journey we could have made to meet with Fiona in Culcairn for the funeral.
Fiona bravely travelled alone from Melbourne.
How she did this is a lesson in resilience and fortitude.
I have to say that most of the funeral, the ceremony and the things said did not relate to J.
He was the most fuss free person and this ceremony seemed overly religious for the person he was.

Nothing seemed real.
We were just trying to get through this terrible day.

Balloons were released at the burial and that added nothing to the day.
I think of J often, I've come to the conclusion that for J to take his own life, there was some terrible sadness that he could no longer deal with.
But who really knows?
I've travelled through his home town Culcairn many times by car and more times on the train going to visit Fiona in Melbourne. I have a chat to him in my mind about happier times spent with him. He's someone I'll never forget.

Over the years I've had parents, grandparents, aunts, uncles, cousins and dear friends pass away and some of these in tragic circumstances, but nothing seemed as bad as the passing of J.

I was never annoyed at him taking his own life, it was more of a case of **Why?**
I respected J as a special person, so I'll leave it at that and perhaps stop thinking **Why?**

Our family shared his life when he studied at Newcastle University. He felt part of our family even when he moved back to the country. If he was ever up our way, he would call in unannounced. He and his mother also visited me when I was at a conference nearer to where he lived.
He was also the king of the Hokey Pokey ice cream!
I've heard it said that suicide is a waste of a life.
I feel this is demeaning to the part of the life the person has already lived.
J did not waste his life, he lived it well, he was a brilliant person with his hands which he could turn to anything.
He was also gentle with a funny sense of humour and just a wonderful man.

Chapter 13

aunty christine's story

Aunty Christine is Mum's sister. Being only fourteen years older than me, I've always seen her more like my big sister than an aunty. She is the gold standard for Aunties. She is wise, has impeccable taste in music and art and has a never-ending wellspring of compassion and love. Her words about J I will cherish as well, and her point about the horrors that some Catholic Priests committed on people in their care is typical Aunty Christine: forthright and to the bone.

J came into our lives when Fiona commenced her degree of a Bachelor of Industrial Design degree. It was the second year that the course was offered at The University of Newcastle. From memory, there was an intake of nineteen students and this circumstance brought them quite close together. Often, Fiona would bring home a group of them to work and Fiona's Mum, unflustered by having a gathering of young people arrive on her door step, would produce lunch and any other sustenance needed.

At the commencement of first semester, J was living out of his car while procuring accommodation. This situation was not conducive for writing assignments and completing assessable tasks. One of the lecturers took J to task over his tardiness in producing an assignment. Fiona, not to be one to tolerate unfairness and willing to speak up for a cause, defended J. and made the lecturer aware of J's homeless state.

Increasingly the extended family crossed paths with J at Fiona's home. He was a friendly young man with an openness to his face and a ready and natural smile. It was with ease that everyone in the family started to build a relationship with J and enjoy his company. Fiona's maternal grandfather and uncle enjoyed gatherings when J was present. They were practical men who could repair motors, weld, fibreglass and solve practical problems and so could J. But there was more to J, he showed an interest in you and the world and possessed a sense of humour. He was a good fit for the family and we liked him. As years rolled on he became much loved by all. There were occasions over that time when we met J's parents, heard stories of J's life and theirs, strengthening the friendship between the two families. It was a happy celebration joining J and his family and friends to mark his 21st birthday. The event was held at a picturesque rural setting and some of the local bovines sought to partake in the festivities. It added more colour to the celebration.

We were sad when Fiona and J completed their studies and Fiona landed a job in Queensland and J returned to his parents' farm. We felt sad that J was not moving on to a career opportunity. Here was a clever young person with so many skills and talents and there was no business or company that offered a position at that stage. We worried how J felt having spent that time and money in achieving his degree and he was returning to the farm. We can only guess at the emotions he experienced but we certainly felt for him. And we were sad about the challenge of a long-distance relationship for he and Fiona in two different states. We were always hopeful when we heard that Fiona and J were together. We wanted them to be together.

The years passed hearing the comings and goings of the relationship. Then came the terrible news of J's suicide. Obviously, we didn't know him to the depth Fiona did, but we couldn't believe he had taken his life. Here was a person with so much to offer and, we thought, to live for. Of course, we tried to understand and guess at what drove J to this decision. It made sense to J but not to us. We never heard the contents of the letter he left for his family. We can only believe that natural and open smile hid happenings, emotions and suffering that J could no longer endure.

I accompanied Fiona's mother and sister on a long and sad journey to attend J's funeral. It was one of the hardest drives that I have had to do, being confronted with the realities of J's passing and the grief being suffered by Fiona, J's family and friends. I wanted to be there as much for J as for Fiona. I couldn't believe that I would never see J again, it was surreal. In my mind, this was not how J's story ends. I had no words for Fiona when we met up at the rural township.

The funeral and burial the next day just made me angry. The church service to me was impersonal, devoid of J's personality and the delivery of the service by the priest lacked emotion. It was just the theatre of the Catholic Church. From that experience, I was determined that when the time came for my aging parents to be farewelled that I was not going to have someone who didn't know them speak about them. I would tell their story, there would be tears and laughter, stories that people knew and could relate to. I would paint a picture of the person.

The burial was the next happening that angered me. I am not a fan of burials and, not being of the Catholic faith, up until then I didn't realise that if you are a Catholic and you commit suicide, you can't be buried in the Catholic section of the graveyard. To maintain the rage, I could well ask, 'Where will the Catholic priests who sexually abused children be buried?' I could not believe that this so-called Christian religion could cast out one of their flock who was suffering so intensely that he took his life.

It is often said after the death of a loved one, 'Life goes on whether you want it to or not'. Fiona's extended family was scattered, and we didn't see the intensity of the effect J's suicide had on her or his family and other friends, but they all had to work through it and face the realities and demands of day to day life. We knew that the impact on Fiona would be great due to the depth of their relationship and its longevity as well as the way he died. We also knew that Fiona is a very strong person. She would find a way forward.

J lingers on in our hearts and memories.

He still features in conversations and he is truly missed. I hope that he has found his peace. We continue to wonder at his suicide and find it incredibly sad that he felt there was no one he could share his burden with and seek help, that he felt he had to shoulder it alone. Obviously asking J, 'Are you Ok?' as we are encouraged to do now would not have been enough for him to reveal his secret, deep troubles.

I am proud of the way that Fiona has been able to work through it and find positive outcomes, from her time with J and the love they shared, in her life now.

And for us, J will remain that friendly young man with the open face, the ready and natural smile who continues to be loved.

Chapter 14

emma's story

My sister Emma was close to me throughout my relationship with J. I fled to see her in the dark, cold months that followed his death as she was one of the few I could bear to be around in all my emotional glory. She is the ultimate sister. Staunch. Funny. Smart. Kind. A fierce defender of those she loves. And a mad dachshund lover.

J adored Emma. He taught her how to waltz. He would pick her up from the Thursday night shift at the nearby department store. He always asked after her when he returned to the farm after university. Emma is right with what she shares. He belonged to our family and we belonged to him.

Writing stuff down has never come very easily to me, ever. This is even more difficult and something I truly wish I wasn't writing about. The thing I remember most and the overwhelming feeling for me at the time was shock. I certainly didn't know how to process what he had done; all I knew was that I had to be there for my sister. I had no idea what to say or really how to help, I just wanted to take her pain away, though I knew I wouldn't be able to do this and it was so hard to see her so sad. I knew she was suffering, but she seemed so brave to me as well. I don't know how she was managing to keep functioning and getting out of bed every day.

I was probably concentrating on my sister, rather than anything else, as that was something that would keep my mind occupied, rather than giving what J had done too much thought. I found that whenever I allowed myself to think about it, my thoughts were all very selfish towards him and that's not the type of feelings I wanted to have about J and what he had done.

It felt like he belonged with our family, we were fortunate Fiona brought him into our lives and that we had a chance to know him.

CHAPTER 15

anon's story

Anon's story is at once both heartbreaking and beautiful.

My uncle 'A' was born with a neurological disorder called Tourette Syndrome. It's a disorder that causes your brain—and body—to do things you can't control. Things like shaking, shuddering, having facial tics and spasms, shouting randomly, or saying words over and over.

My uncle had an extremely severe case of Tourette. He tried everything to control his symptoms—therapy, medication, saw all kinds of specialists. Nothing helped very much.

Very few people understood his condition. When he'd have a fit of symptoms in public, people often assumed he was "crazy" or "drunk." Neither was true. He was constantly bullied, questioned, mocked, and stared at. He was often asked to leave public spaces like restaurants and movie theatres. ('Sir, I must ask you to leave, you're disturbing the other guests.') He was arrested on multiple occasions, which was so traumatizing and humiliating for him.

Uncle A would have given anything to control his symptoms—but there was literally nothing he could do. He described it to me like sneezing. Once he told me, 'When you have to sneeze, you have to sneeze. You can suppress it for a second or two, but eventually it's got to come out. It's not something you can stop.' His Tourette tics were like that.

My uncle tried his best to lead a "normal life" (I use "quotes" because really, what is "normal"?). And he was a tremendously cool human being. He was brilliant and creative. He wrote a book about his experiences with

Tourette's. He was hired to speak and educate audiences about Tourette Syndrome. He loved music. He played the drums. He had a wicked sense of humour.

One of his Tourette symptoms was shouting curse words uncontrollably: 'Shit!' 'Fuck!' 'Asshole!' One day, when I was about seven or eight years old, he was driving me around in his car and he started having a cursing fit. That day, we made a deal: any time he said a curse word, I could say one, too. He told me not to tell my parents. But around him, I could curse all I wanted. It would be our little secret. I thought this was pretty damn cool.

When he died, there was so much confusion. His cause of death was a bit mysterious. It appeared to be a prescription drug overdose. But was it intentional—or an accident?

At the time, he was taking dozens of pills every day—medication for depression, meds for anxiety, meds for obesity (he was clinically obese at this point), meds for pain, meds for muscle spasms, and I don't even know what else. Tons of meds.

As more of the story unfolded, we learned that he had been going around to different doctors, getting excessive refills on his pills, and lying to doctors about the pills he was already taking. So, his death appeared to be pre-meditated. Or at least, partly. We will never know for certain.

We do know that he was in a very dark place, in so much physical and emotional torment, feeling so hopeless about the future. It was clear that he wanted to stop feeling the pain. He wanted to go away—to be free of his body, which so often felt like a prison.

I don't remember much about the first twenty-four hours after he died. It's all pretty foggy. I was pretty young when he died. I think around eleven or twelve. I really didn't know what to think. The whole thing felt so surreal.

My most vivid memory was watching my Mum collapse into hysterical tears, dissolve into one of her relatives at the funeral. I had never seen her cry like that before. Distraught, animalistic sobbing.

She wanted to know, 'Is there anything we could have done to prevent this from happening?' Perhaps she thought she could have done "more" to help her little brother. Perhaps she could have "saved" him.

My guess is, unfortunately, there's probably nothing that anyone could have done.

My uncle was born into the world carrying a very heavy burden, and he carried that burden with grace for as long as he could. And then one day, he threw up his hands and decided, 'That's enough. I want peace. I want to rest.' That's what I believe happened. I am not angry with him for leaving his physical body. I never was. I just hope he's finally experiencing the deep rest and peace that he wanted for so, so long.

And sometimes, when I shout 'FUCCCCK!' in frustration, I smile and imagine that Uncle A is right with me, cursing even louder, and then cracking up with laughter. Us, laughing hysterically at the messy, bizarre, beautiful, unfair, and crazy journey of life.

CHAPTER 16
the suicide slipstream checklist

THE FIRST 24 HOURS

- Ask for help.
  Call at least one supportive friend or family member and tell them as much as you need or want to and make sure you mention this: 'I need your help right now … are you okay for me to call on you and visit with as I need to? Please remember to tell me that I'll be okay … but just not right now.'
  You're going to need immediate and ongoing support, this is you telling someone what you need.

- In Australia, keep this number at hand: Lifeline 13 11 14.
  This is not just for people who might be thinking of ending their life, it's also for people suffering anxiety and depressive episodes and for the bereaved. It's a 24-hour hot line staffed by compassionate, caring people who are happy to talk or listen. Particularly useful when it's the middle of the night and you're going out of your mind.

- Set up a phone tree.
  Depending on your relationship to the person who suicided, you might have to make a number of calls to inform other loved ones. It's exhausting to have to bear the repeated questions, disbelief, and grief. Share out the responsibility to others who can make calls as well. Try to

avoid breaking this news via text message or social media. Death is the one time a personal touch is needed and not an Instagram filter.

- **Find a safe and warm place you can be.**
  Remove yourself from work or obligations as soon as you can. You don't have to give long explanations, answer any enquiry with, 'I've just found out 'X' has died and I need to attend to this.'

- **No drugs, no booze.**
  Nothing that you reach for in order to stop the pain.
  You have to feel it my love, in order to move through it.

- **Get comfortable.**
  It's unlikely that you will sleep much if it all. Set yourself up in a comfortable place and write it out, listen to music, do a few soothing yoga poses, drink some tea, go for a walk in a safe place if you can, even loops around the back yard.

- **Cry. Or don't cry. Wail. Let it all go.**
  Take a breath.
  Then another.
  Then another.
  All you have to do is just take another breath, that's it for now.

THE FIRST WEEK

- Order a food delivery from a supermarket of both fresh food and prepared meals to keep you nourished. Also, this can be delegated to a friend or family.

- Depending on your relationship with the deceased … contact the funeral home and make plans. There may be instructions regarding what the deceased wanted when, or there may not be. Just do your best, you won't be marked on it. If you're not the immediate family, offer to help with arrangements, all offers of meaningful help will be gratefully received even though it may not seem so at the time.

- Contact the coroner or police to get details surrounding the death. Make notes. It will be helpful when you need to refer to information later when you're stuck in the loop of WHY.

- Make arrangements to take time off work, studies and all commitments you can shed. Many pharmacies can write doctors certificates so take that as an option if you can't get in to see your GP.

> AVOID ANYONE WHO ANNOYS YOU, TRIGGERS YOU, FRUSTRATES YOU OR WANTS TO EXPLAIN AWAY YOUR PAIN.

- Surround yourself with understanding, caring types. This is your time to process what you're going through.

> PUT THAT LIFELINE NUMBER IN YOUR PHONE AND USE IT.

- If you see a therapist or have a trusted health professional, make an appointment so you can be honest about how you're feeling and gather support.
- Ask for help with kids, work, study, running the house … yes, it would be lovely for people to know exactly what you need but at times like this, everyone is at a loss to know what exactly to do that will help, so use your words and soak up that support.

> YOUR SLEEP WILL BE STILL SCATTERED, NAP WHEN YOU CAN.

- Do some daily movement even if it's just doing laps around the back yard or push ups at the base of your bed. Move that energy.

KEEP CRYING AND WAILING.
LET IT COME, EVEN IN PUBLIC.
DON'T PUSH IT DOWN.

- Write it out—your feelings, your emotions—the good and the stuff that makes you recoil. Later this will become so important to see how far you've come as you move out of the suicide slipstream.

KEEP BREATHING.

THE FIRST MONTH

- This is where the immediacy of support people starts to wane, not because they don't care but because people want to return to the safety and surety of normal life as soon as possible. It's scary and unpredictable being so raw in the aftermath of suicide, but keep reaching out, keep using your words to ask for help. Mourning someone who has been lost through suicide is not wrapped in a tidy time frame. This is the suicide slipstream and you're going to be in it for a while. Get okay with this new normal.

CRY AND WAIL AS REQUIRED.

- Continue to move your body on a daily basis, aim for some sweat, it's alchemy for your broken heart and spirit.

- You might find it helpful to devote some time each day to having a full-on meltdown. Give yourself say, twenty minutes to rage, release the guilt and sob madly and then at the end of the twenty minutes, just like you would end meditation, pick yourself up and get on with the day.

ESTABLISH ROUTINES.
MAKE YOUR BED.
FLOSS.
PAY YOUR BILLS.
CALL ONE PERSON YOU LOVE EACH DAY.

Take all the "thinking" out of what you should do next or how you should fill your day and rely on feeling into it to carry you through.

KEEP BREATHING.

acknowledgements

THANK YOUS AND LOVE LETTERS

Books don't just appear on the page magically, in my case there was a very strong tribe of cheerleaders, midwives, and truth tellers to support me during the writing process. And not make me feel like a dick for having this idea in the first place.

To the Divas,
    Thank you for doing your best work so I could have creative time to draw this book out.

To the Land Mermaids,
    Thank you for cheering me on, no matter what I'm struggling with and no, I still don't know what you mean when you talk about sales funnels.

To Victoria,
    You're the coach with the most. Thank you for stopping me from buying click funnels and getting me to focus on doing my best work.

To Donna, Claire, Suzanne, Linda, Shirley, Andrea and Becca,
    You're my OG Melbourne mavens … you were all around me when J died, and your collective love carried me through the slipstream.

To the North Shore women's squad especially Emma, Renai, Cate, Karyn, Jan, Lizzie, Liz, Selina, Janet and Koach Kim,

I got a Trojan Horse when I joined the club. I just wanted to row a bit better than I was. I got that (still refusing to pause around the back turn, but, whatever) ... but you also made me a better person and I love youse all.

To Mystic Medusa, Kelly Surtees and Tali of the Astrotwins,
When you have Scorpio in your twelfth house you need ALL the Astro support you can get. These mavens are the best.

To my lovely editor Natasha Gilmour,
Thank you for fashioning my words into something readable and being a force of nature in your encouragement.

To the awesome Nicola Newman,
Thank you for lighting the creative spark within me after all this time away from the paint brush and pen with your painting retreats and heartfelt conversations. Thank you also for my tagline "the mourning after".

To my family,
You held the line through the toughest time of my life and have never let go.
So much love for you.

To my writing retreat buddies,
I marvel at my dumb luck for kicking off the years 2018-2020 in the best possible way. Hanging out with some of the most interesting, encouraging and kindest people I've ever met. The retreat is one of my most favourite memories ever and the thought that I was twerking to "HUMBLE" by Kendrick Lamar at 8 am on a Hilo balcony still tickles me. You are all so dear to me. Thank you will never be enough.

To Alex Franzen,
No lie, without Alex, this book wouldn't be out of me and onto the page. I've followed Alex's amazing work for yonks and if you're not already on her newsletter list or haven't bought her books, STOP, DROP AND ROLL YOURSELF TO THE NEAREST SMARTPHONE / TABLET / LAPTOP / DESK MOUNTED MAGIC BOX THAT CONNECTS TO THE INTERWEBS AND SIGN UP FOR EVERYTHING HERE: http://

www.alexandrafranzen.com

I signed up to do a writing retreat early in 2018, in Hawaii, with Alex. When I signed up, I had zero clue what I wanted to write about. On the pre-retreat call together, still no clue. On the plane to Hawaii? It was an idea wasteland. It wasn't until Madeline, one of the other retreat participants, outlined to the group what she was planning to work on, that idea landed. It was time to write about J and suicide.

Alex is the best of all people. Her heart is open, she is wickedly funny, she deeply cares for the people around her and she introduced me to Butti Yoga. I'll be forever in her debt for the retreats, who she is in this world of craziness and how she's a force of kindness.

To Natalie Green,
    Thank you for reading this book and suggesting ways to improve it. Your encouragement was truly appreciated.

To Dr Melanie,
    Thank you for your care and patience in reassembling the shattered parts of me.

To Alisha Brunten of Love Indigo Creative,
    You created a wonderful home for my words and watercolours. Thank you.

To Kate Lyness,
    Thank you for helping me get this book out into the world and for being my cheerleader.

To you, the reader.
    Thank you for picking up this book. Like I said in the introduction, I wish this was a book you didn't have to read.
    I hope you're doing Ok.
    I hope you're treating your heart, mind and soul with kindness.
    I hope you're emerging from the suicide slipstream and onto firmer shores.
    With much love, Fiona.

HI, I'M FIONA JEFFERIES

On the advice of Alexandra Franzen (when that goddess gives some of her insights, TAKE IT), who was the first person to read this book and say, 'Keep going, this could help someone,' I knocked out this small book, *A Short Book About Suicide* while in Hawaii in 2018. It was about damn time to write about J and suicide.

J's suicide had taken up too much real estate in my head for too long and I'm glad / relieved / cautiously clenching my butt cheeks that these words are now going out in the world to perhaps help someone else navigating the suicide slipstream. Perhaps that person is you.

When I'm not writing thigh slappers about suicide I'm running an all-female design and construction firm in Sydney, bitching about getting up early to go row on the Lane Cover River at 5.10am, baking slutty brownies and worshipping at the Church of Rock.

I also love dachshunds.

If you'd like to share your thoughts on this book and if it helped you in any way, I'd love to hear it. Reach me at fiona@fionajefferies.com.au.

Be kind to yourself and others. You're doing great, keep swimming to safer shores out of the suicide slipstream.

www.ingramcontent.com/pod-product-compliance
Lightning Source LLC
Chambersburg PA
CBHW041500010526
44107CB00044B/1517